Tim
Berners-Lee

Read These Other Ferguson Career Biographies

Maya Angelou
Author and
Documentary Filmmaker
by Lucia Raatma

Leonard Bernstein
Composer and Conductor
by Jean F. Blashfield

Shirley Temple Black
Actor and Diplomat
by Jean F. Blashfield

George Bush
Business Executive
and U.S. President
by Robert Green

Bill Gates
Computer Programmer
and Entrepreneur
by Lucia Raatma

John Glenn
Astronaut and U.S. Senator
by Robert Green

Martin Luther King Jr.
Minister and
Civil Rights Activist
by Brendan January

Charles Lindbergh
Pilot
by Lucia Raatma

Sandra Day O'Connor
Lawyer and
Supreme Court Justice
by Jean Kinney Williams

Wilma Rudolph
Athlete and Educator
by Alice K. Flanagan

Tim
Berners-Lee

Inventor of the World Wide Web

MELISSA STEWART

Ferguson Publishing Company
Chicago, Illinois

Photographs ©: AP/Wide World Photos, cover, 29, 30, 14, 34, 45; Liaison Agency/Catrina Genovese, 8; Liaison Agency/Hulton Getty, 11; Corbis/Underwood & Underwood, 12; Archive Photos/Reuters/Jeff Christensen, 14; Corbis/Bettmann, 16; Liaison Agency/Simon Grosset, 18; Corbis/Adam Woolfitt, 20; CERN/Laurent Guiraud, 22; Corbis/Henry Horenstein, 26; Archive Photos, 28; Archive Photos/Deborah Feingold, 31; Corbis/Catherine Karnow, 38; CERN, 48, 54, 58, 90; Liaison Agency/S. Kermani, 51; Corbis/Adam Woolfitt, 60; Corbis/Robert Holmes, 65; Liaison Agency/William Stevens, 67; SciNetPhotos/Hank Morgan, 72; Corbis/Reuters NewMedia, Inc., 74; Corbis/Julie Houck, 77; AP/Wide World Photos/Thomas Lee, 84; Archive Photos/Reuters/Grahman Earnshaw, 92; Archive Photos/Reuters/Mark Cardwell, 94; Corbis/Kevin R. Morris, 98; Archive Photos/Jeff Greenberg, 101.

An Editorial Directions Book

Library of Congress Cataloging-in-Publication Data
Stewart, Melissa.
    Tim Berners-Lee: inventor of the World Wide Web / by Melissa Stewart.
    p. cm.—(A Ferguson career biography)
    Includes bibliographical references and index.
    ISBN 0-89434-367-X
    1. World Wide Web—History—Juvenile literature. 2. Berners-Lee, Tim—Juvenile literature. 3. Computer programmers—Biography—Juvenile literature. [1. World Wide Web—History. 2. Berners-Lee, Tim. 3. Computer programmers.] I. Title. II. Ferguson career biographies.

TK5102.4 .S74 2001
025.04—dc21
[B]   00-049040

Copyright © 2001 by Ferguson Publishing Company
Published and distributed by
Ferguson Publishing Company
200 West Jackson Boulevard, Suite 700
Chicago, Illinois 60606
www.fergpubco.com

Y-3

CONTENTS

1 THE GREATEST INVENTION
OF ALL TIME 9

2 THE EARLY YEARS 15

3 THE INTERNET AND
HYPERTEXT 27

4 THE BIRTH OF THE WEB 49

5 THE GROWING WEB 61

6 SETTING STANDARDS   **71**

7 BUILDING THE CONSORTIUM   **85**

8 IMPROVING THE WEB   **93**

TIMELINE   **103**

GLOSSARY   **105**

**HOW TO BECOME A
COMPUTER PROGRAMMER**   **108**

**TO LEARN MORE ABOUT
COMPUTER PROGRAMMERS**   **118**

**TO LEARN MORE ABOUT TIM
BERNERS-LEE AND THE
WORLD WIDE WEB**   **120**

INDEX   **124**

Tim
Berners-Lee

Worldwide communication. Tim Berners-Lee works to make the World Wide Web easy for everyone to use.

THE GREATEST INVENTION OF ALL TIME

When you learn about history, you probably have trouble imagining what life was like for people who lived 500, 200, 100, or even 50 years ago. What would it be like to cook every meal over an open fire? What if indoor plumbing, automobiles, and refrigerators didn't exist? It wasn't so long ago that people couldn't toss a bag of popcorn in the microwave, pop a video into the VCR, and then watch their favorite movie at home while enjoying hot, buttery popcorn. Your parents probably didn't have a microwave oven or a VCR when they were your age, and your grandparents may remember a time when there was no television.

People are inventing new things all the time. Most inventions make life a little easier, but a few change the way we live in major ways. Many people say that one of the greatest inventions of all time was the brainchild of Germany's Johannes Gutenberg, who lived in the 1400s.

At that time, all books were written by hand. There were no computers with word processors and no typewriters. If someone wanted a copy of a book, he or she had to copy every single word. As a result, very few people knew how to read, and even fewer owned books. There were no newspapers and no magazines. People got information from a town crier who walked through the streets and sang out the latest news at every corner.

Johannes Gutenberg changed all that when he invented the printing press. Blocks containing the shapes of the letters of the alphabet could be moved around to spell out the words and sentences and paragraphs that appeared on the page of a book. When workers rubbed ink over the letters and used a big roller to press paper on top of them, they could make many copies of a page in a very short time.

Johannes Gutenberg (right) and his partner, Johann Fust. The printing press was a remarkable invention.

Compared to printing out ten copies of a document on a modern laser printer, Gutenberg's printing press took a long, long time to do its job. But it was a big improvement over making one copy at a time by hand.

As time passed, many people refined and improved Gutenberg's basic idea. Eventually, dozens of competing newspapers popped up in every city,

The Gutenberg printing press. This invention made it easier to create books and other publications.

and books could be found in every home. People could easily find out what was happening in their town and around the world every day. They could also enjoy the works of great poets and novelists. Gutenberg changed the way people live in a very important way.

Johannes Gutenberg died more than 500 years ago. Since that time, many other inventions have become a part of our lives. But it is only in the past few years—in the time that you have been alive—that a great invention has been introduced. Many people think it will become as important as the printing press

What is this incredible new object? Actually, it's not an object at all. It's something that you can see and use every day, but it's not something you can touch, and it takes up no physical space. What is it? It's the World Wide Web, and a computer scientist named Tim Berners-Lee invented it.

Like Johannes Gutenberg, Tim Berners-Lee started out with a rough idea of something that would make his life easier and improve the way people share their ideas with one another. In a few short years, Tim's idea blossomed into something that most people cannot imagine living without.

Eric Schmidt of Novell. He believes that the work of Tim Berners-Lee has changed the world.

According to Eric Schmidt, the chief executive officer of a computer company called Novell, "If [computer networking] were a traditional science, [Tim] Berners-Lee would win a Nobel Prize. What he's done is that significant."

THE EARLY YEARS

Tim Berners-Lee was born in London, England, on June 8, 1955. His parents, Conway Berners-Lee and Mary Lee Berners-Lee, had both earned degrees in mathematics from prominent universities in England. They met while working on the Ferranti Mark I, the first commercially available general-purpose computer ever built.

Mary Lee Woods, as she was known before she married, had joined the Ferranti Mark I team in 1951. At first, she helped program the machines. Then, when the earliest models were sold, she helped install them. Conway, who was one of the first members of the British Computer Society, began work on the project in 1953. The couple married a year later.

Conway and Mary Lee taught Tim, his two brothers, Peter and Mike, and his sister, Helen, to think for themselves. They sometimes challenged their children with math games at the dinner table. Tim

A Ferranti Mark I. Tim's parents met while working on such a computer in England.

told a reporter, "We . . . learned to enjoy mathematics wherever it cropped up, and learned that it cropped up everywhere."

Although Mary Lee gave up full-time work to raise her family, she continued to do some computer-programming projects from home. To encourage her children's creativity and imagination, she kept a variety of art supplies on hand at all times. She went to great lengths to teach her children to respect other people and all living creatures. One visitor remembers that the family went so far as to hang long cotton threads in the bathtub to help stranded spiders climb up the sides.

Early Influences

As a child, Tim pretended to build computers out of cardboard boxes and enjoyed leafing through the withered pages of a Victorian encyclopedia titled *Enquire Within Upon Everything*. As a teen, he fell in love with electronics. Two teachers at Emanuel School, a small private school in southwestern London, further fueled Tim's interest in math and science.

Tim describes chemistry teacher Daffy Pennel as a man who "couldn't contain his excitement for chemistry and anything related to it." He fondly remembers that math teacher Frank Grundy often had a twinkle in his eye as he explained mathematical principles. Grundy impressed his students by calculating the answers to complex problems in his head faster than the young mathematicians could work them out on paper.

Arthur C. Clarke. Young Tim was influenced by the work of this science-fiction writer.

Tim Berners-Lee: Inventor of the World Wide Web

When Tim wasn't studying, he enjoyed reading science fiction. One of his favorite stories was "Dial F for Frankenstein" by Arthur C. Clarke. The idea that a similarity exists between the network of neurons in our brains and the mass of cables and wires that make up a computer network intrigued him. In the story, he recalls, there is a "point where enough computers get connected together" to create a system that "started to breathe, think, and react autonomously." The idea of a computer system acting on its own fascinated Tim, and he thought about it for many years.

After graduating from Emanuel School, Tim enrolled in Queen's College, one of several undergraduate schools at Oxford University. He decided to major in physics. Looking back, Tim says, "Physics was fun, and in fact a good preparation for creating a global [computer] system." Both physicists and computer programmers try to develop very basic rules and principles that can be scaled up to explain how large systems behave, such as a planet in outer space or a bit of data in cyberspace.

Although Tim wouldn't realize it until much later, one of his most important early influences was John Moffat, a physics tutor at Oxford. Tim recalls:

Queen's College at Oxford University. Tim was a physics major at this school.

. . . when I brought him a problem I had worked out incorrectly, using a strange technique and symbols different from the well-established ones, he would not only follow my weird reasoning to find out where it went wrong, but would then use my own strange notation to explain the right answer. This great feat involved looking at the world using my definitions, comparing them with his, and translating his knowledge and experience into my language.

John's ability to recast his own thinking and see the world through Tim's eyes made quite an impression on his young student. Years later, Tim would think about John Moffat as he was designing a system for standardizing the way searches are conducted on the World Wide Web.

During his time at Oxford, Tim was finally able to make one of his childhood fantasies become a reality. He rounded up an old television set, some spare parts, and a soldering iron, and he built his first real computer.

After graduating from Oxford University in 1976, Tim went to work for a telecommunications company in Poole, England. Two years later, he moved to

A view of CERN from the air. This physics laboratory in Geneva was the stage for much of Tim's early work.

a company in Ferndown, England, and began writing computer software programs. By 1980, Tim had decided to become a computer consultant. One of his first clients was the European Center for Nuclear Research (CERN), a physics laboratory near Geneva, Switzerland.

Developing Enquire

When large-scale changes were made in CERN's computer system, it was Tim's responsibility to notify researchers who were affected. He would show the scientists how to access their data. Although Tim was a computer whiz, he was not so good at remembering names and faces. He had trouble keeping track of which researchers were working on which projects and what kind of computer each person was using.

For Tim, the solution was obvious—he would create a computer program that could make up for his bad memory. The program would have a weblike structure that could quickly and easily provide Tim with all the files pertaining to a particular researcher's work. When Tim entered a researcher's name, the program could access all the relevant files—even if they were stored on a variety of computer systems or had been created by different people.

With just a few taps on his computer keyboard, Tim could draw together all the relevant information regarding the researcher's projects and computer needs. The program was unique because it was able to make random associations—just like a human brain. Tim named his program Enquire because its organizational structure reminded him of the Victorian encyclopedia he had enjoyed so much as a child.

Tim didn't know it at the time, but Enquire contained the conceptual basis for the World Wide Web—a revolutionary computer program he would write a decade later. Looking back on Enquire, Tim told a reporter that it could keep "track of all the random associations one comes across in real life and brains are supposed to be so good at remembering, but sometimes mine wouldn't."

After six months, Tim left CERN. He gave his program to a co-worker, but no one else at CERN understood its value. The disk and its contents sat on a shelf and collected dust. Between 1981 and 1984, Tim worked for Image Computer Systems. He completed a variety of projects, including some that involved writing graphics and communications software. Although he enjoyed his work, Tim decided to apply for a fellowship so that he could return to CERN. His proposal was accepted, and he soon headed back to Switzerland.

An exciting time. When Tim was a young man, the computer world was going through major changes.

THE INTERNET AND HYPERTEXT

While Tim was working at his first few jobs, the world of computer hardware was undergoing a radical transformation. The computer his parents had built in the 1950s was a huge machine that took up an entire room. Even in the 1960s and early 1970s, few computer scientists could imagine that people might want to use a computer at home. Only highly skilled professionals working at colleges, hospitals, government offices, and other large organizations operated these complicated machines.

Filling up a room. In the 1950s, computers were huge, complicated machines.

That attitude began to change in the late 1970s. In 1977, Apple Computers introduced the Apple II to the world. It was advertised as the first "complete, ready-to-use personal computer." It came neatly enclosed in a plastic case and even offered

Steve Jobs and the Apple II. This computer was intended for personal use by everyday people.

The Internet and Hypertext

The IBM personal computer. This machine was introduced in 1981.

color graphics to its users. In 1981, International Business Machines (IBM) released its own personal computer.

In 1983, Microsoft Corporation introduced Microsoft Word—a powerful word-processing program—and Windows—a program that allowed users to work on more than one document or program at the same time. By using a mouse, people could

Bill Gates of Microsoft. The inventions of Microsoft Word and Windows changed the way people used computers.

The Internet and Hypertext 31

The beginning of computer use. The first personal computers were bigger and harder to use than they are today.

point at and click on the information they needed. These innovations made computers much easier for the average person to use. By the late 1980s, families were starting to buy personal computers, and more and more children were learning to use them.

The Internet

While the young, energetic computer geniuses at Apple and IBM were busy designing and developing the first personal computers, workers at the Advanced Research Project Agency (ARPA) were improving the worldwide network of computers we now know as the Internet. In the 1960s, the ARPA had been created by the U.S. Department of Defense to develop a computer networking system that would not be jeopardized if a few key government computers were destroyed by nuclear weapons.

This seemed like an important goal because, at that time, the United States was in the midst of a Cold War with the Union of Soviet Socialist Republics (USSR). Although the two nations were not technically at war, each believed that a "hot" fighting war might break out at any moment. While the two rivals openly competed for technological dominance in space and in industry, they secretly trained military troops and stockpiled nuclear weapons.

When the Soviets launched *Sputnik 1* in 1957, the implications were very clear to everyone in the

Sputnik I. *The people of the Advanced Research Project Agency were concerned about this Soviet satellite.*

United States. If the USSR could send a satellite to space, it could also propel a nuclear warhead to a target on the other side of the world. While the U.S. National Aeronautics and Space Administration (NASA) raced to design and build spacecraft that could carry astronauts first into space and then to the Moon, the ARPA raced to develop a network that would protect America's computer systems.

Today we think of the Internet as a vast network of computers connected by miles of wires and cables. With the click of a mouse, computers at opposite ends of the world can communicate at lightning speed, exchanging documents, pictures, sounds, games, and programs. But the early Internet was slow and cumbersome. For many years, only a few government employees and university researchers used it.

Even after electronic mail (e-mail) was invented in 1972, few people found the Internet useful. However, all that changed in 1989 when a thirty-four-year-old computer scientist named Tim Berners-Lee came up with an incredible idea. By this time, Tim was back at CERN, and he wanted to create a way for researchers all over the world to share their data and work together more easily. "I thought, look, it would be so much easier if everybody asking me questions all the time could just read my database, and it would be so much nicer if I could find out what these guys are doing by just jumping into a similar database of information for them," recalls Tim.

What Is Hypertext?

The solution Tim came up with involved combining the Internet and something called hypertext. What is hypertext? It's easier to recognize than it is to define. The word *hypertext* is used to describe all the writing you see when you look at a Web page. Like the text in a book, hypertext is a series of words that convey a thought or idea. But hypertext does more than text written on paper.

As you read a Web page, you occasionally encounter words that are underlined or colored. When you see these hyperlinks, you can use your mouse to drag the cursor on top of the highlighted text until the arrow turns into a hand with a pointing finger. Then, with a single tapping motion, you can access additional information that is somehow related to the original text.

That single mouse click may call up a different

part of the same document, or it may begin an electronic search for an entirely new document. Either way, the new information usually appears in the blink of an eye. Highlighted words are not the only kinds of hyperlinks that can access additional information. Clicking on a photograph or icon can also call up other documents, movies, or sound recordings.

If you look up *hyper* in the dictionary, the first definition you will read is "above, beyond." Hypertext goes above and beyond the text in a book, a magazine, or a newspaper by allowing the person who writes it to make random connections to other things that he or she finds interesting. The writer can thus take ideas and concepts from a wide range of sources and seamlessly link them together so that a reader can access them quickly and conveniently.

Writing hypertext is a bit more complicated than writing regular text in a word-processing program. Besides stringing letters together to create the words, sentences, and paragraphs that appear on a Web page, a hypertext author must also write a computer code that specifies how to find the linked documents, photographs, and other elements. In

A world of Web sites. Web designers work to make Web pages attractive, informative, and easy to use.

addition, the code provides instructions for putting all the pieces together.

Many different kinds of computer languages are used to write code. A hypertext author uses hypertext markup language (HTML) or its newer cousin extensible markup language (XML). HTML controls the hyperlinks on a Web page. It also tells you where different elements are positioned when a Web page appears on your screen. For example, HTML tags organize the text on a Web page into headings, paragraphs, and lists. Some commands determine how hyperlinks are highlighted. Other coding instructions designate the placement of photographs, and still others allow you to watch videos and hear sound recordings.

```
BHTML>
<\<>HEAD<\>>
<\<>TITLE<\>>NASA
Homepage<\<>/TITLE<\>>
<\<>META HTTP-EQUIV="pragma" CON-
TENT="no-cache"<\>>
<\<>/HEAD<\>>

<\<>BODY
BACKGROUND="/images/bg_tile3.gif"
ALT="Gray background tile used for
layout" BGCOLOR="#FFFFFF"
TEXT="#000000" LINK="#000099"
VLINK="#003366"
ALINK="#99CCFF"<\>>

<\<>TABLE WIDTH=600 BORDER=0 CELL-
PADDING=0 CELLSPACING=0<\>>
<\<>TR VALIGN=TOP<\>>
<\<>TD ALIGN=CENTER WIDTH=600<\>>
```

The HTML code used to write the NASA Web page

Once written, hypertext allows a reader to choose how he or she will navigate through each Web page and the entire Web site. The goal of hypertext is to give the reader options. Readers will follow different paths depending on their personal interests.

For example, if you go to the NASA Web site, *http://www.nasa.gov/,* you'll find dozens of different hyperlinks.

The NASA home page

While the link leading to the "Just for Kids" section of the Web site might be your first choice, someone who is planning a vacation might be more interested in the "Visiting Nasa" link.

If you decide to click on the "Just for Kids" hyperlink, you will soon be faced with a variety of new choices. Do you want to learn more about planets and other objects in space or would you rather

The "Just for Kids" section of the NASA Web site

view information about the people who make the space program a reality? Only you know the answer.

If you click on the "Visiting NASA" hyperlink, you will have even more decisions to make. Do you want to learn about the Air and Space Museum of the Smithsonian Institute? Would you like to find out when the next space shuttle will launch? You could go to each of these links—in any order you wish—or you could choose to go

The Visiting NASA section of the NASA Web site

back and view information about astronauts instead, or you could decide to go to a completely different Web site. The decision is yours to make. All the information is there waiting for you, just a few keystrokes away.

"Hypertext is like the nation's system of highways and roads," says noted screenwriter and film critic Charles Deemer. "There are many ways to get from the West Coast to the East Coast, depending on whether or not we are in a hurry, depending on what kind of scenery we want to look at, depending on what may intrigue us as a side trip from moment to moment. . . . Hypertext is [also] like life itself, full of choices and consequences, full of forks in the road."

Hypertext and the Human Mind

It is not surprising that Charles Deemer sees a connection between hypertext and the way we experience life. After all, it is our minds that interpret the world we live in. As your senses present you with information about your surroundings, your brain decides how to respond. It makes choices based on memories of past experiences and on things you have learned in school and from other people.

For instance, if your fingertips touch a hot door-knob, a message travels to your brain, which instantly pulls up a dozen or more bits of seemingly unrelated information. They flash through your mind: your mother's gentle warning, "Hot, hot, burn the baby"; the pain of the mild burn you received when you did not heed her warning; a campfire; a fire scene from a movie or TV show; and the firefighter who came to your school and taught you to "Stop, drop, and roll." These memories quickly help you make sense of the situation. In a microsecond, you realize that there may be a fire on the other side of the door. You know you should leave the building and call 911. Because you have all those memories, you make the choice that keeps you safe.

Most modern computer scientists, including Tim Berners-Lee, like to compare hypertext to human memories and the Internet to the network of neurons that make up the human nervous system. Nearly two decades before the ARPA began thinking about how to make the Internet a reality, one man was already thinking about hypertext. In 1945, Vannevar Bush envisioned a system that could link related information or ideas through "trails." He

Dr. Vannevar Bush. This scientist had important ideas about how the human mind links pieces of information together.

described his ideas in an article that appeared in *Atlantic Monthly* magazine.

Bush's inspiration was—quite simply—the human mind. In the article, he says, the mind "operates by association. With one item in its grasp, it snaps instantly to the next that is suggested by the association of thoughts." Bush suggested that humans would benefit tremendously from an information-retrieval system that could make random connections between seemingly unrelated subjects.

A Global Hypertext System

Twenty years later, in 1965, Ted Nelson, a software designer and writer, coined the term *hypertext* to describe Bush's concept. Nelson envisioned a kind of global hypertext system, but he never came up with a truly user-friendly way to make it work. That's where Tim Berners-Lee came in.

In his book, *Weaving the Web*, Tim says, "I happened to come along . . . after hypertext and the Internet had come of age. The task left to me was to marry them together." And that is exactly what Tim did. He took a powerful but complex communication network that only the elite could use and turned it into a mass medium. "The Web made the Net useful because people are really interested in information and don't really want to have to know about computers and cables," Tim explains.

Robert Cailliau. This Belgian scientist was Tim's colleague at CERN and supported him in his work.

THE BIRTH
OF THE WEB

By 1989, Tim had a compelling vision and a rough idea of how to transform the Internet into a workable, useful system, but he knew that was not enough. To develop and launch what we now know as the World Wide Web, Tim would need the support and assistance of his colleagues at CERN.

According to standard procedure at CERN, he would have to submit a proposal and get it approved before the lab would endorse the project. Over the next few months, Tim wrote a paper suggesting that all CERN's computer resources be linked by an Internet-based information-sharing system that he would create. He also explained that—pending the success of that system—it would eventually go global.

Although Tim's proposal did not get the reception or the funding he had hoped for, his supervisor, Mike Sendall, felt the idea had merit. He let Tim devote time to his pet project. Tim had also captured the imagination of Robert Cailliau, a Belgian engineer who had worked at CERN for nearly twenty years. Because Robert was widely known and respected at CERN, he found a way to get Tim many of the resources he needed: student helpers, money, machines, and office space. As soon as the most important piece of equipment—a NeXT computer—was approved by Mike Sendall, Tim really got to work.

The NeXT computer was a very sophisticated piece of hardware for its time. Despite NeXT's superior operating system and other software and hardware advances, it failed to gain widespread acceptance. The machine itself is no longer manufactured. However, its operating system, NeXTSTEP, can be used in a number of applications. Tim found the computer to be invaluable.

The NeXT computer. Tim found this piece of equipment to be essential to his work.

Building a Browser

First, he needed to find a way to view hypertext documents that had been sent over the Internet. Initially, Tim hoped to modify an existing hypertext system into a Web browser that could open and display hypertext documents. Unfortunately, he had trouble finding a company that could understand his overall vision. One major problem was the scope of what Tim had in mind. He wanted to develop an open-ended, global system with no central manager or database.

At that time, the people developing hypertext systems believed that a central database was essential. How else, they asked Tim, could a system keep track of all its hyperlinks? They pointed out that if a hypertext system has no central database and a document is deleted, all the links from other documents will go nowhere. In other words, there will be "dangling links." Only a system with a central database can routinely check for deleted documents and then erase all the hyperlinks to documents that no longer exist.

Tim acknowledged these drawbacks in the hypertext system he was proposing. But as far as he was concerned, it would be impossible to create a self-monitoring program that could accomplish his primary goals. Although less than ideal in some respects, "Letting go of the need for consistency was a crucial design step that would allow the Web to scale," Tim explains. And this is the reason that when you use the Web today, you occasionally get a frustrating "Web Site Not Found" message when you click on a link.

As Tim later told a reporter from *Time*, "this dangling-link thing may be a problem, but you have to accept it." But the developers could not see Tim's point of view. In the end, Tim realized that he would have to build his own Web client—a computer program for creating, editing, and browsing hypertext documents. The browser part of the program would allow users to request and view linked documents.

Tools of the Trade

Once Tim had a clear vision of how his Internet-based data-transfer system should work, it was relatively easy for him to devise the tools he needed to make his Web client program—which he named WorldWideWeb—work. Besides HTML, Tim developed hypertext transport protocol (*HTTP*),

At the computer. Tim created many of the tools that today are familiar parts of surfing the Web.

which is a standard set of rules used to convey hypertext documents across the Internet. When you click on a hyperlink, the Web browser on your computer uses HTTP to ask the host computer—the computer with the linked file on its hard drive—to transmit the data file to your computer. As soon as the hypertext document arrives, the browser follows HTML instructions to assemble and display the Web page for you.

A "Web page" is any hypertext document that is

being viewed through a browser. A "Web site" is a group of Web pages posted on the World Wide Web by one person, institution, or company. The introductory page to a Web site is called a "home page." The term can also be used to describe the first page your Web browser reads off the Web when you log on, or it can be a page that you have created yourself.

Tim also realized that—in his system—every Web page would need a unique address, or uniform resource locator (URL). According to the strategy he developed, each part of a URL contains information about the individual or group that created the hypertext document and the computer that is hosting the Web site.

For example on NASA's Web site, you'll see that *http://kids.msfc.nasa.gov/Rockets/Living.asp* is the URL for a Web page that describes what life is like for astronauts on board the space shuttle. The first part of the address, *http*, is the abbreviated form of "hypertext transport protocol." As you already know, it is the set of rules used to access and retrieve a document that has been written in HTML. When *http* appears at the beginning of a URL, the Web browser knows it will receive an HTML document.

Web browsers can also understand other types of protocols. For example, the prefix *ftp* stands for file transfer protocol (FTP), the set of rules most commonly used to transfer non-hypertext files across the Internet before Tim invented HTTP. By making the first Web browser compatible with FTP, Tim allowed early Web users to access established Internet news groups and previously existing Internet articles.

The second part of a URL is called the domain name. It tells you about the computer that runs the Web site. For example, in the domain name *kids.msfc.nasa.gov/Rockets/Living.asp*, the letters *msfc* stands for "Marshall Space Flight Center." Workers at this Alabama-based branch of NASA created and now update all the information in the "Just for Kids" area of the space agency's Web site. The second half of the domain name, *nasa.gov*, tells you that the computer hosting the Web site is owned by NASA, a U.S. government agency.

Not all domain names end with *gov*. Web sites sponsored by private companies end in *com*, while Web sites sponsored by nonprofit organizations end in *org* and Web sites sponsored by colleges and universities end in *edu*. The domain suffix *mil* indicates a military Web site, and *net* appears at the end of all network Web site URLs.

The next part of the URL, *Rockets*, tells NASA's host computer where the data file for the hypertext document is located on the computer's hard drive. The last part of the URL, *Living.asp*, is the name of the actual data file. The *asp* suffix stands for "active server page." It is a computer language that allows the author to include small programs called scripts in the Web page. Scripts allow the author to create some dynamic elements on the page, such as the moving cartoon at the top right of the "Living in Space Web" page. These kinds of fun features cannot be created with plain HTML.

Up and Running

Once Tim had created a Web client, HTTP, HTML, and the URL document addressing system, he needed just one more thing: software that could store data files containing hypertext documents and that would allow a browser to access and retrieve hypertext documents when a user requests them. Eventually, this Web server software would be loaded onto powerful host computers with high-speed, permanent connections to the Internet. In

1990, however, Tim ran both the server program and his WorldWideWeb client program on his NeXT computer.

Using the client program, Tim had soon constructed the world's first Web page. It included his notes on various projects as well as the specifications for HTML, HTTP, and URLs. By the end of

A bright future. By the early 1990s, Tim Berners-Lee was enjoying both the professional and personal parts of his life.

1990, the system was up and running on two computers.

Tim's overall objective had not changed. He still wanted to develop a global system. Compared to this lofty goal, the Web's first practical application was rather mundane. After loading a simple browser onto every computer at CERN and converting the lab's telephone directory to a hypertext document, the system allowed everyone at CERN to access the information simply and easily—no matter what kind of computer they were using. In the grand scheme of things, using the system in this way may have been a baby step—but Tim knew he was on the road to real progress.

Around this time, another kind of baby steps became an important part of Tim's life. At the beginning of 1991, he and his wife, Nancy Carlson, welcomed their first child into the world. Nancy is an American who had moved to Europe to work for the World Health Organization. She met Tim at an acting workshop.

In early 1991, Tim's future looked very bright—personally and professionally. He looked forward to watching both his new daughter and his brainchild, the World Wide Web, grow and mature.

The University of Helsinki in Finland. It was here in April 1992 that a group of students created a browser called Otherwise.

THE GROWING WEB

For years, the engineers and physicists at CERN had been facing the challenges of computer incompatibility. In many cases, people using other kinds of computers could not access documents written or data compiled on one computer. Tim knew that the Web offered the perfect solution to this problem. It could retrieve and read information created by different software programs or stored on machines with different operating systems.

While the strengths of the system were obvious to Tim, Robert Cailliau, and a few others, most people at CERN were slower to embrace the Web. Although Tim had released the WorldWideWeb program to all CERN employees with NeXT computers, many people simply could not see its tremendous potential.

The Web Goes Global

By August 1991, however, a few high-energy physics researchers at other institutions had shown interest in Tim's system. He gladly provided them with the tools they needed to get the Web up and running. Despite this interest, Tim decided that his system might find stronger supporters outside the physics research community. Therefore, he released his original WorldWideWeb program for creating and editing Web pages, a simplified browser that had been created by a student assistant named Nicola Pellow, and a server. Although the WorldWideWeb program could be used only on a NeXT computer, the browser and server could be loaded on any computer. Now that these components were available—free of charge—on the Internet, many more people had access to them. Tim also posted notices on Internet newsgroups so that people would know how the components could be used.

One of the newsgroups Tim chose was alt.hypertext, which is geared toward people with a strong interest in hypertext. "Putting the Web out on alt.hypertext was a watershed event," recalls Tim in his book *Weaving the Web*. "It exposed the Web to a very critical academic community. I began to get e-mail from people who tried to install the software. They would give me bug reports, and 'wouldn't it be nice if . . .' reports. And there would be the occasional, 'Hey, I've just set up a server, and it's dead cool. Here's the address.'"

Finally, Tim was getting real feedback. The positive comments helped make him more enthusiastic than ever about his brainchild, while the negative ones helped him refine and improve the system. "The people of the Internet built the Web, in true grassroots fashion," says Tim. As more and more faceless people contributed ideas, Tim decided that it would be helpful to create an Internet newsgroup, called comp.infosystems.www, that dealt specifically with questions and comments about the Web.

As greater numbers of people were exposed to the Web, enthusiasm for the system snowballed. "The most valuable thing happening," recalls Tim, "was that people who saw the Web, and realized the sense of unbound opportunity, began installing the server and posting information. Then they added links to related sites that they found were complementary, or simply interesting. The Web began to be picked up by people around the world."

A Better Browser

Although the Web was starting to catch on, Tim realized that its growth was being limited. Although the primitive, general-purpose browser could be used by anyone on any computer, only people using a NeXT computer could see all the Web's bells and whistles. Tim wanted to create a browser that was a bit more flashy and a lot more user-friendly for people using a variety of computers. He knew this was the key to generating widespread interest in the Web.

Because Tim did not have enough funding to hire a team of computer scientists to develop a superior general-use browser, he posted Internet notices suggesting that creating a Web browser would be an excellent student project. A group of students at the University of Helsinki in Finland saw one of Tim's messages and liked his idea. By April 1992, they had developed a browser called Erwise. A month later, a student at the University of California at Berkley

The University of California at Berkeley. The browser ViolaWWW was invented by a student here in May 1992.

released ViolaWWW, a Web browser that could display HTML with graphics and animations.

Like Nicola Pellow's primitive browser, neither of these new browsers had writing and editing functions. They could be used to retrieve hypertext documents but they could not be used to create them. This fact had a tremendous effect on how the Web developed and on how it is used today. Although Tim envisioned the Web as a means of improving communication and collaboration, it is used primarily as a tool for gathering information.

Still, these new browsers helped the Web grow in new directions. The number of people accessing Tim's server was doubling every three or four months. By January 1993, there were about fifty Web servers worldwide, and new browsers were popping up all over the place.

One of these, called Arena, was developed by Dave Raggett, a programmer who worked for Hewlett-Packard in Bristol, England. According to Tim, Dave "was convinced that hypertext Web pages could be much more exciting, like magazine pages rather than textbook pages, and that HTML could be used to position not just text on a page, but pictures, tables, and other features. He used Arena to demonstrate all these things . . . "

Meanwhile, Marc Andreessen, a student at the University of Illinois in Urbana, and Eric Bina, a staff member at the university's National Center for Supercomputing Applications, had seen ViolaWWW.

Marc Andreesen. He worked on the browser called Mosaic and went on to found Netscape Communications Corporation.

They were so impressed by it that they decided to create their own browser—Mosaic.

While other browser developers had been content when their program worked, Marc Andreessen was not. He wanted more. He wanted his browser to be used by as many people as possible. Each time the team released a new version of their program, Marc encouraged users to give him feedback. He worked late into the night adding all kinds of special features that people had requested.

As a result of all this input, the Mosaic browser was simple to download and easy to install. Most important, a person had almost nothing to learn before using it to navigate through the Web. Mosaic quickly became the browser of choice. However, like ViolaWWW, Arena, and Erwise, it could only be used on computers with Unix operating systems. It could not be used on PCs or Macintoshes—the kinds of computers most people had sitting on their desks at work and in their family rooms at home.

That's where Tom Bruce came in. As the co-founder of the Legal Information Institute at Cornell University, he understood the benefits of the Web and the needs of lawyers. Because most lawyers worked on a PC in their office, he had written a browser called Cello for Microsoft Windows—the most common operating system for PCs. "For the first time," says Tim, "people could see the Web in its multicolor, multifont glory on the world's most widespread computer platform."

Tim was very impressed with Cello—and with Tom Bruce. The two quickly discovered that the Web was not their only common interest. Years earlier, Tom had worked as a stage manager at a theater. Although Tim's experience with the theater was strictly amateur, the two men enjoyed discussing ideas about theatrical lighting and audiovisual equipment.

Tim told Tom Bruce that he was scheduled to meet Eric Bria and Marc Andreessen and invited him to come along. At the meeting, Tim suggested that the programmers modify Mosaic to include writing and editing options, but Eric and Marc did not seem interested. Tim was disappointed. The meeting had not gone as well as he had hoped.

In addition, he was becoming increasingly concerned about what the National Center for Supercomputing Applications was telling the media. They seemed to be suggesting that Mosaic and the World Wide Web were one and the same. Were they trying to seize control of his invention? Tim became even more worried when the center launched projects to adapt Mosaic for both PCs and Macintoshes.

SETTING STANDARDS

By the summer of 1993, the rate of people connecting to the CERN server was doubling every three or four months. The number of "hits" per day had risen steadily from 100 in 1991 to 1,000 in 1992 to 10,000 in 1993. At this point, Tim was very pleased with his success, but he started to give serious thought to the issue of standardization.

The Internet Engineering Task Force had already officially agreed to standardize Web addresses using Tim's original URL naming scheme. However, Tim continued to worry

Handling success. Tim knew that the Internet needed to grow in a way that would help everyone use it.

Tim Berners-Lee: Inventor of the World Wide Web

about the universal compatibility of browsers and servers.

As more and more people developed these important Web components, Tim feared that developers might decide to branch off in new directions. This could end up fragmenting his worldwide system. Perhaps, he thought, the Web needed some kind of unbiased governing body that could guide its future development and make sure that its initial objectives were not violated.

Over the next few months, Tim discussed this idea with several groups. He talked to his colleagues at CERN and an assortment of Web pioneers at a WWW Wizards Workshop held in Cambridge, Massachusetts. He also consulted Michael Dertouzos, director of the Laboratory for Computer Science at the Massachusetts Institute of Technology as well as representatives from Digital Equipment Corporation. Most seemed to agree that a consortium—a group made up of people from all the major companies with interests in the development and evolution of the Web—would be the most effective kind of supervisory organization.

Michael Dertouzos. This scientist from MIT was among the people that offered Tim advice and ideas about the World Wide Web.

From Mosaic to Navigator

Meanwhile, the National Center for Supercomputing Applications had released two versions of the Mosaic browser. One Version could be used on any PC, and another version that could be used on the Macintosh. As Tim expected, the browsers captured the imagination of the public and the media. In fact,

Tim Berners-Lee: Inventor of the World Wide Web

these browsers were so user-friendly and became so universally successful that most popular Web browsers today are based on Mosaic.

In April 1994, Marc Andreessen and some of his colleagues left the University of Illinois and formed Netscape Communications Corporation. By December, the company had completed work on Netscape Navigator, a Web Browswer that would eventually make Marc Andreessen one of the Web's first millionaires. In fact, when Netscape began selling its stock to the public the following year, twenty-four-year-old Marc Andreessen was suddenly worth $58 million.

Netscape knew that other companies were also developing browsers. "They released their product for free, so it would be picked up widely and quickly," said Tim, describing their bold reasoning. They decided that if they could launch their product first and it "was widely and rapidly accepted, then the company would have a platform from which to launch other products for which it would charge money," continues Tim. "It would bring millions of people to Netscape's home page. . . . There, Netscape could display ads from companies that would pay to reach a large viewership."

This clever business strategy worked just as Netscape had hoped. Today, Netscape Navigator is one of the two most widely used Web browsers in the world. Its only serious competition is Microsoft's Internet Explorer.

Surfing the Web

A person who is actively requesting or reading Web pages through a browser, such as Netscape Navigator or Internet Explorer, is said to be "surfing the World Wide Web." There are many ways to request Web pages. If you know the URL, you could type the whole thing into the white box at the top of your browser. But because many URLs are long, it may be easier to type in just the URL of the Web site's home page and then use links to get to the Web page you want.

For example, you could type in the address *http://kids.msfc.nasa.gov/Rockets/Living.asp* but that is long and cumbersome. So you could type in *http://www.nasa.gov* and click on hyperlinks for the "Just for Kids Web" page, then the "Pioneers & Astronauts" Web page, and finally the "Living in Space" Web page. Then, if you want to return to the

"Pioneers & Astronauts" Web page or any other previously viewed Web pages, you could use the arrows in the upper left-hand corner of the browser's window to move backward and forward.

If you think you may want to go back to a particular Web page or Web site later, you can use your browser to create a "bookmark" or to add it to your

Surfing the Web. Computer users find that there are many ways to access information on the Internet.

list of favorite Web sites. Or you might choose to print out the pages instead.

If you are looking for a particular kind of information, but have no specific Web page or Web site in mind, you could use a *search engine*—a program that allows you to search for Web pages containing words you specify. For example, if you are doing a report on anteaters, you could use a search engine to look for "anteater" in every Web page posted on the World Wide Web. The home pages of most modern Web browsers give you easy access to one or more search engines. You can also access them by typing their addresses into the white box at the top of your Web browser. Here's a list of some of the most commonly used search engines and their URLs:

Search Engine	Address
About.com	*http://www.about.com*
Alta Vista	*http://www.altavista.com*
Excite	*http://www.excite.com*
Go.com	*http://www.go.com*
Infoseek	*http://www.infoseek.com*
Hot Bot	*http://www.hotbot.com*
Lycos	*http://www.lycos.com*

Tim Berners-Lee: Inventor of the World Wide Web

Of course, before you can surf the Web, you must have access to the Internet. To get Internet access, you will need a computer, a modem, and an account with an Internet service provider. Until recently, all modems sent data over phone lines, but today they also work over digital data lines and the same underground cables that transmit cable television. An Internet service provider will charge you a fee to temporarily connect, or log on, to its server and use the Internet. The company will also send you browser software so that you can retrieve and view Web pages.

Everyone with an Internet account has a unique personal address. The first part of the address is called the user ID, or user name. Some user IDs include part of the person's name or a fun word that he or she has chosen. It is followed by the @ symbol, which means "at." Like Web URLs, Internet addresses end in a domain name that includes the name of the host computer running the account and the same kinds of suffixes as URLs. For example, an Internet account for a woman named Jane Brown might begin with the user ID jbrown. If she has an account with American Online, a popular Internet service provider, her Internet address would be *jbrown@aol.com.* Even the president of the United States has an Internet address. You can find him at *President@whitehouse.gov.*

The World Wide Web Consortium

While the computer scientists at Netscape were developing their revolutionary browser, Tim was working on a creation of his own—the World Wide Web Consortium, or W3C. Although many people were wondering whether Tim would cash in on the Web—as the founders of Netscape had—this was not what he had in mind. He admits that, in 1992, he and Robert Cailliau had considered starting a company. But by 1994, Tim says his main concern "was to make sure that the Web I had created continued to evolve." In *Weaving the Web*, he writes,

> *My motivation was to make sure that the Web became what I'd originally intended it to be—a universal medium for sharing information. . . . I wanted to see the Web proliferate, not sink my life's hours into worry over a product release. [If I directed a consortium,] I'd be free to really think about what was best for the world, as*

opposed to what would be best for one com-
mercial interest. I'd also be free to wield a per-
suasive influence over the Web's future
technical directions.

For Tim, the decision was clear. He would give up the road to riches and, instead, continue to nurture his brainchild. "Core in my upbringing was a value system that put monetary gain well in its place, behind things like doing what I really want to do," adds Tim. When asked about Tim's decision, Robert Cailliau jokingly told a reporter, "Tim's not after the money. He accepts a much wider range of hotel-room facilities than a CEO would."

Throughout early 1994, Tim continued to discuss starting a Web consortium with MIT's Michael Dertouzos and Al Vezza. All three men agreed that given the Web's international appeal, the consortium should have two headquarters—one in the United States and one in Europe. MIT would be the U.S. headquarters, and CERN would be the European headquarters.

When summer arrived, Tim once again decided to evaluate the number of hits his server at CERN was receiving daily. In the past year, the number had continued to grow at the same unbelievable rate as in previous years. By now, approximately 100,000 people were connecting to the server each day.

Tim was amazed by the progress. He told reporters that watching the Web's growth gave him "an incredibly good feeling." He also said it was "a lesson for all dreamers . . . that you can have a dream and it can come true."

Four years earlier, Tim had looked forward to living through the growing pains of both the Web and his newborn daughter. Now, as the number of Web users continued to expand, so did Tim's family. In June, Nancy gave birth to the couple's second child—a son. Tim was elated.

A month later, MIT agreed to sponsor the World Wide Web Consortium. They offered Tim a job and asked when he could start. By September, Tim and his family had left their home in the French countryside and taken up residence in Massachusetts. The plan was for Tim to lead the American branch of the consortium, while Robert Cailliau, Mike Sendall, and François Fluckiger were left in charge at CERN.*

In a 1995 article, the *New York Times* described the consortium and the role Tim plays:

The consortium's membership numbers more than 100 and includes the major software companies trying to find riches on the Internet— Microsoft, I.B.M., the Oracle Corporation, Sun Microsystems, Silicon Graphics Inc., the Netscape Communications Corporation, and others. Working groups and committees are formed to make recommendations about Web standards. But in the end, Mr. Berners-Lee decides.

---

* A few months later, CERN decided not to act as the consortium's European headquarters. It was replaced by the National Institute for Research in Computer Science and Control in France. In 1996, Keio University in Japan became the consortium's Asian headquarters.

Sharing his thoughts. Tim has spent much time speaking to groups about the World Wide Web.

BUILDING THE CONSORTIUM

T im had been thinking about how he wanted the Web consortium to be structured for quite a while. Now it was time to get down to business. Over the next few months, he began to put together a group that would oversee the Web's future development. The consortium would gently steer the Web in new directions, and Tim was glad to be in the driver's seat. In *Weaving the Web*, Tim writes:

> *[The] consortium's purpose was [always] to 'lead the Web to its full potential.' I wanted an*

atmosphere that would allow individuals, representing their companies or organizations, to voice their personal ideas and find ways to reach common understanding. . . . A small, core staff housed at the Laboratory of Computer Science [at MIT] and sites in Europe and Asia would produce specifications and sample code, which members—and anyone else, for that matter—could pick up and use for any purpose, including commercial products, at no charge.

Digital Equipment Company, Netscape, Hewlett-Packard, and IBM were among the first companies to join the consortium. Today, there are almost 500 members. At periodic meetings, consortium members discuss and agree upon new common computer protocols, such as the Platform for Internet Content Selection (PICS). PICS lets parents and teachers filter out Web sites they feel are offensive or inappropriate for children. It can also direct a user's attention to sites that may be of particular interest to the user.

Developing standards is important. It is the best way to ensure that the same Web can be accessed by everyone—no matter where they live, no matter what kind of computer they have, no matter what kind of browser they use, no matter who their Internet service provider is, and no matter which search engines they prefer. "The Web needs to be a system in which everyone can participate equally," says Tim.

One of the consortium's primary objectives is to prevent the Web from fragmenting into many smaller Webs. If the consortium did not exist, there is a possibility that one company might try to seize control of the standard protocols that govern the Web's operations. Tim gave the following example to a reporter from *Technology Review*:

> *A company could start by releasing Web browser software and make it available free or at very low cost, to capture the vast majority of the market. Later, that company decides to introduce a feature in this product that can be taken advantage of only if the designer of the Web page deviates from accepted Web standards in some fashion. A Web user would then suddenly begin encountering pages that read, "Sorry, you need software from Company X to enter this site."*

Anyone who slaps a "this page is best viewed with Browser X" label on a Web page appears to be yearning for the bad old days, before the Web, when you had very little chance of reading a document written on another computer, another word processor, or another network. And once a browser vendor has established such a monopoly, it has an incentive to continue to make arbitrary changes to the [actual] standard, forcing potential competitors to play an endless game of catch-up. All the other bright ideas at all the other software companies are stifled because they have to be compatible with a "standard" that changes at one company's whim.

To prevent this from happening, the World Wide Web consortium asks all the major companies involved in Web development to sit down together and agree on standards. Tim tries to make the companies see that by working together, everyone can profit. While the example described here might seem tantalizing, Tim points out that the monopoly company could ultimately end up getting burned if all the other companies band together and decide to move in a different direction. "There is always an incentive for one company to try to move standards, to change standards and leave other companies inoperable," Tim told the *World Wide Web Journal*. "But there's a tremendous incentive for the community as a whole to prevent that."

Directing the Consortium

Although Tim has the ultimate say in what the consortium does, he is more interested in discussing issues and finding common ground than in wielding his power. "Tim leads by his vision," says Carl Cargill of Netscape. "And if you disagree with his vision, he will talk to you and talk to you until he agrees with your vision or you agree with his—or both of you come to a new vision."

Tim's attitude in leading the consortium closely matches the beliefs of the religion he has adopted. Although he was raised as an Anglican, Tim rejected Christianity as a teenager because its teachings are not compatible with science. Now he considers himself a Unitarian Universalist.

According to Tim, his church believes in "the inherent dignity of people and in working together

A special vision. As leader of the World Wide Web Consortium, Tim makes the effort to explain and discuss his ideas.

to achieve harmony and understanding." Unitarian Universalism "tackles the spiritual side of people's lives and of values and of the things you need to live your life, but it doesn't require you to believe six impossible things before breakfast," he adds with a smile. It is a setting in which people think, discuss, argue, and try to be accepting of differences of opinion and ideas. Tim would probably describe the World Wide Web consortium in a very similar way.

*Around the world. By the mid-1990s, access to the Internet was
becoming more and more common.*

IMPROVING THE WEB

8

hroughout 1995, the consortium continued to grow, and so did the Web. By 1996, everyone in the United States had heard of the Web—and many of these people were connected at home, at work, or both. Tim watched with fascination as the Web grew and evolved. In some ways, it became exactly what Tim had originally envisioned. But in other ways, it moved further and further away from what he had in mind.

Tim had hoped the Web would become a "communications tool that would enable small groups to work more efficiently in teams." But because browsers and editors evolved separately rather than as two functions performed by a single Web client, creating a Web page involved a lot more work than Tim expected.

As a result, he says, "Content is produced only by those with enough incentive to learn to write HTML. [The outcome has been that] World Wide Web sites have tended to be corporate sites, corpo-

Taking a look. In 1996, these New Yorkers tried out the Internet at a mobile lunch truck in Manhattan.

rations talking to consumers, rather than groups wondering what they're going to have for lunch."

"In the prototype," Tim adds, "you could create a link without having to write any code. You'd just browse around, find something interesting, go back to the thing you were writing, and then just make a click on a hot key, and it would make a link for you automatically." In other words, adding a link would be as simple as clicking on the "print" or "save" icons on the tool bar of a word-processing program.

Introducing XML

In the late 1990s, the consortium began developing some new tools to help nudge the Web in this direction. In 1998, they released XML—a markup language that has a number of advantages over its cousin HTML. First of all, XML is easier to write and easier to read than HTML, so more people will be able to use it. How could such a program eventually be used? Tim described his ultimate vision to a reporter from *Technology Review*:

> Say that you conduct a meeting as a hypertext document. You start by dragging in a video version of yourself, with real-time sound. You

remind those invited to come by sending them a hypertext e-mail with a pointer to the meeting. To [attend the meeting,] they just follow the link. . . . Some join by audio, and some drag their own video into the document.

People introduce points by writing them into the minutes, making links to background material. At one point in the meeting three people realize they need to discuss something separately, and with a single keystroke, one forks off a new meeting document that they will catch up with later.

According to Tim, all the technology to conduct this kind of meeting already exists—though some of it is still in the early stages of development.

XML was also developed to improve the Web in other ways. For instance, it is better than HTML at handling certain kinds of data. While HTML is good for describing how running text, photos, and icons should be represented on a Web page, it is not ideal for formatting the data in spreadsheets, address books, or financial transactions. However, XML was created with this kind of data in mind.

XML is also more flexible than HTML. Users can

create their own formatting tags to meet their specific needs. This is possible because XML was designed to describe something rather than to perform an action. For example, HTML tags such as < H1 > and < \ < >font color = "red" < \ > > designate that text should be a certain size or color. But XML tags focus on the reason for highlighting text in a certain way. It might use such tags as < \ < >headline < \ > > or < \ < >advertisement < \ > >.

Because this kind of logic is embedded in hypertext documents written with XML, it will eventually be possible to conduct more successful searches in these documents—as long as Web authors follow an established set of rules for naming data fields. This means that if you are doing a report on harp seals, for example, your search engine will find many sites with information about these marine mammals. It will recognize the entire phrase—rather than the individual words. So it will no longer retrieve sites that describe musical instruments or products that have received the *Good Housekeeping* Seal of Approval.

XML also has the ability to retrieve hypertext documents that use different terms to describe the same object or idea. For example, by the time you

Millions of users. Scientists are among the many kinds of people who use the World Wide Web everyday.

are ready to buy your first car, the search engines of the future will be able to deliver Web pages that describe "cars" as well as those with information about "automobiles" and "vehicles." In other words, the Web will possess the same skill as John Moffat, the Oxford physics tutor who impressed Tim Berners-Lee more than twenty years earlier. The Web of the future will better react to the way humans think.

XML is also capable of processing information on the spot. If you are viewing an HTML page from a clothing store's Web site and want to know all the colors a particular shirt comes in, you will have to request the additional information from a computer located at the company's headquarters. That could take some time, and if there is some kind of computer glitch anywhere along the Internet, you may not be able to get the information you want.

However, if the same page had been written with XML, you could retrieve the additional information from a small program embedded in the page's XML format. As a result, you would get the information faster. In addition, there would be less traffic on the Web—so Web pages could be delivered to you, and everyone else, more quickly.

Putting Data in Its Place

In 2000, the consortium introduced another new program that will improve the Web. The Resource Description Framework (RDF) protocol was designed specifically to handle metadata—data that describes other data. Examples include library catalogs that describe publications and photo libraries that contain large collections of scanned images. "The Web is quickly becoming the world's fastest growing repository of data," says Tim. "RDF provides the necessary foundation and infrastructure to support the description and management of this data. RDF can transform the Web into a more useful and powerful information resource."

According to consortium members Jon Bosak and Tin Bray, "RDF . . . should do for Web data what catalogue cards do for library books." In an article for *Scientific American*, they wrote, "Because the Web has no librarians and every Webmaster wants, above all else, to be found, we expect that RDF will achieve a typically astonishing Internet growth rate once its power becomes apparent."

By using XML and RDF together, Tim and other consortium members hope to develop better ways to manage the growing body of information that makes up the Web. These are just a few of the projects the consortium is working on. Its goal is to anticipate potential problems and develop solutions that will keep the Web growing and expanding in the future.

Tim is pleased with the way the consortium is functioning and expects the group to continue creating useful ways to gently guide the Web's future development. Leading the organization is a big job, but Tim is more than willing to keep on doing it. In

A computer generation. The work of Tim Berners-Lee has helped bring information to schoolchildren all over the world.

less than ten years, he has watched his fledgling idea revolutionize the way people communicate and conduct business. He can't wait to find out how the Web will change and grow in future decades—and to see how it will continue to affect the way we live our lives.

TIMELINE

1955 Tim Berners-Lee is born in London, England, on June 8.

1973 Graduates from Emmanuel School in London, England

1976 Graduates from Queen's College at Oxford University in England

1980 Begins a six-month work assignment at CERN, a physics laboratory near Geneva, Switzerland; writes the Enquire software program

1989 Returns to CERN

1990 Develops all the tools (browser, server, HTML, HTTP, URL addressing scheme) needed to create and view Web pages

1991 Daughter is born; makes all Web software available on the Internet

1992 Other people begin to create browsers

1994 Son is born; establishes the World Wide Web Consortium; moves to the United States

1996	Consortium releases the specifications for PICS
1999	Receives the MacArthur Fellowship; consortium releases the specifications for XML
2000	Consortium releases specifications for RDF

GLOSSARY

electronic mail (e-mail)—an Internet messaging system

extensible markup language (XML)—a markup language with a number of improvements over HTML

file transfer protocol (FTP)—the set of rules most commonly used to transfer files across the Internet before HTTP was available

host computer—a computer with the linked hypertext files on its hard drive

hyperlink—highlighted text or other elements in a Web page that call up related Web pages.

hypertext—the written information on a Web page. It contains highlighted text that links to other documents.

hypertext markup language (HTML)—a computer language that a person creating a Web page uses to position the photos, text, and other elements. It also controls hyperlinks on the Web page.

hypertext transport protocol (HTTP)—a standard set of rules used to convey hypertext documents across the Internet

Internet—a worldwide network of computers

modem—a device that allows computers to communicate with one another

newsgroup—an Internet bulletin board that specializes in a particular topic

search engine—a software program that allows you to search for Web pages containing words you specify

uniform resource locator (URL)—the addressing system used to guarantee that every Web page has a unique identifier

Web browser—a computer program that opens and displays hypertext documents

Web client—a computer program used to create, edit, and browse Web pages

Web page—a hypertext document viewed through a browser

Web server—a software program that stores hypertext documents to the hard disk of a powerful computer that has a high-speed, permanent connection to the Internet

World Wide Web—an extensive collection of interlinked hypertext documents that can be accessed through the Internet and viewed on a Web browser

WorldWideWeb—the name of Tim Berners-Lee's first Web client program

HOW TO BECOME A COMPUTER PROGRAMMER

The Job

Computer programmers work in the field of electronic data processing. They write instructions that tell computers what to do in a computer language, or code, that the computer understands. Systems programmers specialize in maintaining the general instructions that control an entire computer system. Maintenance tasks include giving computers instructions on how to allocate time to various jobs they receive from computer terminals and making sure that these assignments are performed properly. There are approximately 648,000 computer programmers employed in the United States.

Broadly speaking, there are two types of computer programmers: *systems programmers* and *applications programmers*. Systems programmers maintain the instructions, called programs or software, that control the entire computer system, including both the central processing unit and the equipment with which it communicates, such as terminals, printers, and disk drives. Applications programmers write the software to handle specific jobs and may specialize as engineering and scientific programmers or as business programmers. Some of the latter specialists may be designated chief business programmers, who supervise the work of other business programmers.

Programmers are often given program specifications, prepared by systems analysts, which list in detail the steps the computer must follow in order to complete a given task. Programmers then code these instructions in a computer language the computer understands. In smaller companies, analysis and programming may be handled by the same person, called a programmer-analyst.

Before actually writing the computer program, a programmer must analyze the work request, understand the current problem and desired resolution, decide on an approach to the problem, and plan what the machine will have to do to produce the required results. Programmers prepare a flowchart to show the steps in sequence that the machine must make. They must pay attention to minute detail and instruct the machine in each step of the process.

These instructions are then coded in one of several programming languages, such as BASIC, COBOL, FORTRAN, PASCAL, RPG, CSP, or C++. When the program is completed, the programmer tests its working practicality by running it on simulated data. If the machine responds according to expectations, actual data will be fed into it and the program will be activated. If the computer does not respond as anticipated, the program will have to be debugged—that is, examined for errors that must be eliminated. Finally, the programmer prepares an instruction sheet for the computer operator who will run the program.

The programmer's job concerns both an overall picture of the problem at hand and the minute detail of potential solutions. Programmers work from two points of view: from that of the people who need certain results and from that of technological problem solving. The work is divided equally between meeting the needs of other people and comprehending the capabilities of the machines.

Electronic data systems involve more than just one machine. Depending upon the kind of system being used, the operation may require other machines such as printers or other peripherals. Introducing a new piece of equipment to an existing system often requires programmers to rewrite many programs.

Process control programmers develop programs for systems that control automatic operations for commercial and industrial enterprises, such as steelmaking, sanitation plants, combustion systems, computerized production testing, or automatic truck loading. *Numerical control tool programmers* program the tape that controls the machining of automatic machine tools.

Requirements
High School   In high school, you should take any computer programming or computer science courses available. You should also concentrate on math, science, and schematic drawing courses, since these subjects directly prepare students for careers in computer programming.

Postsecondary   Most employers prefer their programmers to be college graduates. In the past, as the field was
first taking shape, employers were known to hire people
with some formal education and little or no experience but
determination and aptitude to learn quickly. As the market
becomes saturated with individuals wishing to break into
this field, however, a college degree is becoming increasingly important.

Many personnel officers administer aptitude tests to
determine potential for programming work. Some employers send new employees to computer schools or in-house
training sessions before they are considered qualified to
assume programming responsibilities. Training periods
may last as long as a few weeks, months, or even a year.

Many junior and community colleges also offer two-
year associate's degree programs in data processing,
computer programming, and other computer-related
technologies.

Most four-year colleges and universities have computer science departments with a variety of computer-
related majors, any of which could prepare a student for
a career in programming. Employers who require a college degree often do not express a preference as to major
field of study, although mathematics or computer science
is highly favored. Other acceptable majors may be business administration, accounting, engineering, or physics.
Entrance requirements for jobs with the government are
much the same as those in private industry.

Licensing and Certification   Students who choose to
obtain a two-year degree might consider becoming cer-
tified by the Institute for Certification of Computing

Professionals. (See "To Learn More about Computer Programmers" for contact information.) Although it is not required, certification may boost an individual's attractiveness to employers during the job search.

Other Requirements Personal qualifications such as a high degree of reasoning ability, patience, and persistence, as well as aptitude for mathematics, are important for computer programmers. Some employers whose work is highly technical require that programmers be qualified in the area in which the firm or agency operates. Engineering firms, for example, prefer young people with an engineering background and are willing to train them in some programming techniques. For other firms, such as banks, consumer-level knowledge of the services that they offer may be sufficient background for incoming programmers.

Exploring

If you are interested in becoming a computer programmer, you might visit a large bank or insurance company in the community and seek an appointment to talk with one of the programmers on the staff. You may be able to visit the data processing center and see the machines in operation. You might also talk with a sales representative from one of the large manufacturers of data processing equipment and request whatever brochures or pamphlets the company publishes.

It is a good idea to start early and get some hands-on experience operating and programming a computer. A trip to the local library or bookstore is likely to turn up countless books on programming; this is one field where the resources to teach yourself are highly accessible and available for all levels of competency. Joining a computer club and reading professional magazines are other ways to become more familiar with this career field. In addition, you should start exploring the Internet, itself a great source of information about computer-related careers.

High school and college students who can operate a computer may be able to obtain part-time jobs in business computer centers or in some larger companies. Any computer experience will be helpful for future computer training.

Employers

Computer programmers work for manufacturing companies, data processing service firms, hardware and software companies, banks, insurance companies, credit companies, publishing houses, government agencies, and colleges and universities throughout the country. Many programmers are employed by businesses as consultants on a temporary or contractual basis.

Starting Out

You can look for an entry-level programming position in the same way as most other jobs; there is no special or standard point of entry into the field. Individuals with the necessary qualifications should apply directly to companies, agencies, or industries that have announced job openings through a school placement office, an employment agency, or the classified ads.

Students in two- or four-year degree programs should work closely with their schools' placement offices, since major local employers often list job openings exclusively with such offices.

If the market for programmers is particularly tight, you may want to obtain an entry-level job with a large corporation or computer software firm, even if the job does not include programming. As jobs in the programming department open up, current employees in other departments are often the first to know, and are favored over nonemployees during the interviewing process. Getting a foot in the door in this way has proven to be successful for many programmers.

Advancement

Programmers are ranked—according to education, experience, and level of responsibility—as junior or senior programmers. After programmers have attained the highest available programming position, they can choose to make one of several career moves in order to be promoted still higher.

Some programmers are more interested in the analysis aspect of computing than the actual charting and coding of programming. They often acquire additional training and experience in order to prepare themselves for promotion to positions as systems programmers or systems analysts. These individuals have the added responsibility of working with upper management to define equipment and cost guidelines for a specific project. They perform only broad programming tasks, leaving most of the detail work to programmers.

Other programmers become more interested in administration and management and may wish to become heads of programming departments. They tend to be more people-oriented and enjoy leading others to excellence. As the level of management responsibilities increases, usually the amount of technical work performed decreases, so management positions are not for everyone.

Still other programmers may branch out into different technical areas, such as total computer operations, hardware design, and software or network engineering. With experience, they may be placed in charge of the data systems center. They may also decide to go to work for a consulting company, work that generally pays extremely well.

Earnings

According to the National Association of Colleges and Employers, the average 1999 starting salary for college graduates employed in the private sector was about $40,800. The U.S. Department of Labor reports that median annual earnings for computer programmers were $47,550 in 1998. The lowest 10 percent of programmers earned $27,760, while the highest 10 percent earned more than $88,730 annually. Programmers in the West and the Northeast are generally paid more than those in the South and Midwest. This is because most big computer companies are located in northern California's Silicon Valley or in the state of Washington, where Microsoft, a major employer of programmers, has its headquarters. Also, some industries, like public utilities and data processing service firms, tend to pay their programmers higher wages than do other types of employers, such as banks and schools.

Work Environment

Most programmers work in pleasant office conditions, since computers require an air-conditioned, dust-free environment. Programmers perform most of their duties in one primary location but may be asked to travel to other computing sites on occasion.

The average programmer works between 35 and 40 hours weekly. In some job situations, the programmer may have to work nights or weekends on short notice. This might happen when a program is going through its trial runs, for example, or when there are many demands for additional services.

Outlook

Employment opportunities for computer programmers should increase faster than the average through 2008, according to the U.S. Department of Labor. Employment growth will be strong because businesses, scientific organizations, government agencies, and schools continue to look for new applications for computers and to make improvements in software already in use. Also, there is a need to develop complex operating programs that can use higher-level computer languages and can network with other computer equipment and systems.

Job applicants with the best chances of employment will be college graduates with a knowledge of several programming languages, especially newer ones used for computer networking and database management. In addition, the best applicants will have some training or experience in an applied field such as accounting, science, engineering, or management. Competition for jobs will be heavier among graduates of two-year data processing programs and among people with equivalent experience or with less training. Since this field is constantly changing, programmers should stay abreast of the latest technology to remain competitive.

TO LEARN MORE ABOUT COMPUTER PROGRAMMERS

Books

Gascoigne, Marc. *You Can Surf the Net: Your Guide to the World of the Internet.* New York: Puffin, 1996.

Lampton, Christopher. *Home Page: An Introduction to Web Page Design.* Danbury, Conn.: Franklin Watts, 1997.

Lund, Bill. *Getting Ready for a Career in Computers.* Mankato, Minn.: Capstone Press, 1998.

Pedersen, Ted. *Make Your Own Web Page!: A Guide for Kids.* New York: Price Stern Sloan, 1998.

Perry, Robert. *Personal Computer Communications.* Danbury, Conn.: Franklin Watts, 2000.

Reeves, Diane Lindsey. *Career Ideas for Kids Who Like Computers.* New York: Facts On File, 1998.

Websites

The Computer Museum History Center
http://www.computerhistory.org/
Online archives and exhibits about the history of computers

PC World Online
http://www.pcworld.com
An online magazine that provides news about the computer industry as well as reviews of software and other products

Programmers Heaven
http://www.programmersheaven.com
An online source for computer programmers with all levels of experience

Where to Write

Association for Computing Machinery
One Astor Plaza
1515 Broadway
New York, NY 10036
ACMHELP@acm.org
For more information about careers in computer programming

Institute for Certification of Computing Professionals
2200 East Devon Avenue, Suite 247
Des Plaines, IL 60018
For information on certification programs

TO LEARN MORE ABOUT TIM BERNERS-LEE AND THE WORLD WIDE WEB

Books

Berners-Lee, Tim. *Weaving the Web*. San Francisco, Calif.: Harper, 1999.

Cochrane, Kerry. *The Internet*. Danbury, Conn.: Franklin Watts, 1995.

Kalbag, Asha, editor. *Build Your Own Website*. Newton, Mass.: E D C Publications, 1999.

Kalbag, Asha, editor. *World Wide Web for Beginners*. Newton, Mass.: E D C Publications, 1998.

Lampton, Chris. *The World Wide Web*. Danbury, Conn.: Franklin Watts, 1997.

Wallace, Mark, editor. *101 Things to Do on the Internet.* Newton, Mass.: E D C Publications, 1999.

Websites
History of the Web
http://www.hitmill.com/internet/web_history.html
Features a summary of the Web's development and has links to many other interesting sites

Hypertext Terms
http://www.w3.org/Terms.html#hypertext
Clear, simple definitions in a Web page within the World Wide Web Consortium's site

A Little History of the Web
http://www.w3.org/History.html
A timeline of the major events that led to the development of the Web

Tim Berners-Lee
http://www.w3.org/People/Berners-Lee/Overview.html
Biographical information about Tim Berners-Lee as well as a list of his upcoming speaking engagements and answers to questions that people frequently ask him

World Wide Web Consortium
http://www.w3.org
Background information about the group as well as descriptions of ongoing projects

Interesting Places to Visit

Compuseum: American Computer Museum
234 Babcock Street
Bozeman, MT 58715
406/587-7545
A museum of the history of the information age

The Computer Museum History Center
Building T-12A
Moffett Federal Airfield
Mountain View, CA 94035
650/604-2579
A museum that preserves computing history

Massachusetts Institute of Technology
77 Massachusetts Avenue
Cambridge, MA 02139
617/253-1000
To tour the institute where the WWW Consortium was founded

Museum of Science
Science Park
Boston, MA 02114
617/723-2500
For great exhibits such as Cahners ComputerPlace, the Computer Clubhouse, and the Technology Learning Center

The Computer Museum of America
Colman College
7380 Parkway Drive
La Mesa, CA 91942
619/465-8226
To explore the history of computers and computing

INDEX

Page numbers in *italics* indicate illustrations.

Advanced Research Project
    Agency (ARPA), 33, 35, 44
America Online, 79
Andreessen, Marc, 67–69, *67*,
    75
Apple Computers, 28
Apple II computer, 28, *29*
applications programmers,
    108–109
Arena Web browser, 66, 68
ARPA. *See* Advanced
    Research Project Agency.
alt.hypertext newsgroup, 63

Berners-Lee, Conway (father),
    15–16
Berners-Lee, Helen (sister), 16
Berners-Lee, Mary Lee
    (mother), 15

Berners-Lee, Mike (brother), 16
Berners-Lee, Peter (brother),
    16
Berners-Lee, Tim, *8*, *26*, *54*,
    58, *72*, *84*, *90*
bookmarks, 77
Bosak, Jon, 100
Bray, Tim, 100
Bria, Eric, 69
British Computer Society, 16
Bush, Vannevar, 44, *45*, 46

Cailliau, Robert, *48*, 50, 61,
    81–82
Cargill, Carl, 89
Carlson, Nancy, 59
Cello Web browser, 69
CERN. *See* European Center
    for Nuclear Research.

Clarke, Arthur C., *18*, 19
Cold War, 33
comp.infosystems.www
   newsgroup, 63
computer programmers
   career advancement,
      114–115
   career exploration, 112–113
   educational requirements,
      110–112
   employers of, 113
   employment outlook,
      116–117
   job description, 108–110
   salaries, 115–116
   work environment, 116

Deemer, Charles, 43
Dertouzos, Michael, 73, *74*,
   81
"Dial F for Frankenstein"
   (Arthur C. Clarke), 19
Digital Equipment Corpora-
   tion, 73
domain names, 56–57

electronic mail, 35
Emanuel School, 17
Enquire program, 24
*Enquire Within Upon Every-
   thing* (encyclopedia), 17
Erwise Web browser, 64, 68
European Center for Nuclear
   Research (CERN), *22*, 23,
   25, 35, 49–50, 59,
   61–62, 71, 81

extensible markup language
   (XML), 38, 95–97, 99–101

Ferranti Mark I computer, 15,
   16
file transfer protocol (FTP), 56
Fluckiger, François, 82
Fust, Johann, *11*

Gates, Bill, *31*
Grundy, Frank, 18
Gutenberg, Johannes, 10, *11*,
   13

Hewlett-Packard, 66
home pages, 55
HTML. *See* hypertext markup
   language.
HTTP. *See* hypertext transport
   protocol.
hyperlinks, 36–37, 40–42, 52,
   54
hypertext, 36, 38, 40, 43,
   46, 52, 54–55, 59, 66
hypertext markup language
   (HTML), 38, *39*, 54–55,
   57–58, 94–96, 99
hypertext transport protocol
   (HTTP), 53–55, 57–58

Image Computer Systems,
   24–25
International Business
   Machines (IBM), 30, *30*,
   83, 86
Internet, 33, 35, 44, 46–47,

49, 52–53, 62–63, *77*,
79, *92*, *94*
Internet Engineering Task
Force, 71
Internet Explorer Web
browser, 76

Jobs, Steve, *29*

Kejo University, 83

Laboratory for Computer
Science, 73
Laboratory of Computer
Science, 86
Legal Information Institute, 68

Macintosh computers, 68, 70,
74
Microsoft Corporation, 30, *31*,
76, 83
Microsoft Word, 30
Moffat, John, 19, 21, 99
Mosaic Web browser, 68–70,
74–75

National Aeronautics and
Space Administration
(NASA), 35, *39*, 40–43,
41, *42*, *43*, 55, 76–77
National Center for Supercom-
puting Applications, 67,
69, 74
National Institute for Research
in Computer Science and
Control, 83

Nelson, Ted, 46
Netscape Communications
Corporation, 75, 83, 86
Netscape Navigator Web
browser, 75–76
New York Times newspaper,
83
NeXT computers, 50, *51*, 58,
62, 64
NeXTSTEP operating system,
50
Novell computer company, 14
numerical control tool pro-
grammers, 110

Oxford University, 19, *20*, 21

PCs, 68–70, 74
Pellow, Nicola, 62, 66
Pennel, Daffy, 17–18
Platform for Internet Content
Selection (PICS), 86
printing press, 10–11, *11*, *12*
process control programmers,
110

Queen's College, 19, *20*

Raggett, Dave, 66
Resource Description Framework (RDF) protocol,
100–101

Schmidt, Eric, 14, *14*
Scientific American magazine,
100

search engines, 78
Sendall, Mike, 50, 82
service providers, 79
Sputnik I satellite, 33, *34*
systems programmers,
    108–109

tags, 38–39, 97
Technology Review magazine,
    87–88, 95–96

U.S. Department of Defense,
    33
uniform resource locators
    (URLs), 55, 57–58, 71,
    76, 78
Unitarian Universalism, 89, 91
University of California at
    Berkeley, 64, *65*, 66
University of Helsinki, *60*, 64
Unix operating systems, 68
URLs. *See* uniform resource
    locators.
user IDs, 79

Vezza, Al, 81
ViolaWWW Web browser,
    67–68

Weaving the Web (book), 46,
    63, 80–81, 85–86
Web browsers, 55–56, 64,
    66–70, 74–77
Web clients, 53, 57
Web pages, 36, 39, 54–55,
    96, 99
"Web Site Not Found" error
    message, 53
Web sites, 55, 78, 94–95
Windows operating system,
    30, 69
Woods, Mary Lee. *See* Bern-
    ers-Lee, Mary Lee.
World Wide Web, 13, 24, 47,
    49, 53, 55, 62–64, 70,
    73, 78, 93–95, *98*
World Wide Web Consortium
    (W3C), 80, 82–83, 85,
    87–88, 91, 95, 100–101
World Wide Web Journal,
    89
WWW Wizards Workshop, 73

XML. *See* extensible markup
    language

ABOUT THE AUTHOR

Melissa Stewart earned a bachelor's degree in biology from Union College and a master's degree in science and environmental journalism from New York University. She has been writing about science and technology for almost a decade.